STC Guard Card Training®

Counterterrorism

Published by
Security Training Center,® LLC.
6520 PLATT AVE #174
WEST HILLS, CA 91307-3218
Security-Training-Center.com
(855) 500-3633

Trademarks: "Security Training Center", "STC Guard Card Training", the Security Training Center Logo, and the Guard Card Training logo are trademarks of Security Training Center,® LLC.
"Palladium Education" and the Palladium Education Logo are trademarks of Palladium Education,® Inc.

ISBN-13:   978-1-939408-52-5

10 9 8 7 6 5 4 3 2

Counterterrorism

Alex Haddox, M.Ed.
Author

William Green, M.Ed.
Editor in Chief

Disclaimer

Security Training Center,® LLC. offers course material for training and certification. It is up to the student to complete the training within the mandatory timeframe as required by the state licensing agency. Security Training Center,® LLC. and its parent companies accept no responsibility for loss of licensure, registration, employment or fines resulting from failure of the student to complete the training within the timeframes specified by the state licensing agency.

Security Training Center,® LLC. and its parent companies *will not* notify or remind students of training deadlines. It is up to the individual to maintain personal professional training records, credentials and schedule of courses.

The material contained within this manual is the sole creation of Security Training Center,® LLC. which holds the copyright hereto. It is not official State-created training material.

Security Training Center,® LLC.

Notice of Liability

The information in these programs is distributed without warranty. While every precaution has been taken in the preparation of this program, neither the author, Security Training Center,® LLC. nor its parent companies shall have any liability to any person or entity with respect to any injury, loss, or damage caused or alleged to be caused directly or indirectly by the instructions contained in any program or by instruction provided by Security Training Center,® LLC.

STC Guard Card Training®

About Security Training Center,® LLC.

Security Training Center,® LLC. is a professional security guard training company. The mission of Security Training Center,® LLC is to educate security personnel and organizations in the latest protocols and techniques to keep staff, property, and other valuables safe. A proactive approach to security awareness prevents many problems from occurring thereby reducing risk to staff and potential liability actions. The approach is to teach early identification of potential problems and how to defuse conflicts before reaching crisis. Security Training Center,® LLC's staff and advisory board have decades of experience in military, law enforcement, executive protection, private security, defensive weapons and martial arts.

Not only does Security Training Center,® LLC offer direct training, but also provides guard card training materials for use by other organizations. Many companies have highly trained and experienced individuals. Unfortunately these companies may lack the teaching experience or materials to be able to impart the knowledge. For situations like these, Security Training Center,® LLC. offers pre-packaged STC Guard Card Training® materials. Security Training Center,® LLC's team is comprised exclusively of education and security professionals, many of whom hold advanced degrees in Adult Education and Training.

STC Guard Card Training®

STC Guard Card Training® materials are available in multiple formats to meet most any need:

- Instructor-led, classroom training
  Printed STC Guard Card Training® manuals, lecture notes, handouts and presentations
- Online, self-paced training
  Interactive guard card eLearning with audio, video, and animations
- Podcasts
  Downloadable or streamable audio lectures, case studies, and interviews
- Books
- YouTube videos

Security Training Center,® LLC.
6520 PLATT AVE, #174
WEST HILLS, CA 91307-3218
Security-Training-Center.com
(855) 500-3633

Contents

Objectives

Minimum Length: 4 hours

Facility: Classroom

Required Materials: 1) Counter Terrorism manual
2) Instructor digital presentation
3) Computer
4) Projector or computer-connected display

Objectives

By the end of this lesson, Counter Terrorism, the student will be able to:

- Identify functions of major counterterrorism agencies.
- Describe the nature of terrorism.
- Explain the goals of terrorism.
- Describe the differences between homegrown violent extremists and international terrorism.
- Identify the common homegrown violent extremists and organization goals.
- Identify suspicious behavior.
- Better protect the post from terrorist threats.

Introduction to Terrorism

The threat represented by terrorism is pervasive in our lives, regardless of where one lives. No country or community is immune to attack by lone individuals, terrorist cells, or large-scale direct armed conflict. In the year 2016 a great number of highly publicized terrorist attacks occurred around the world, primarily in the United States and in the allied countries. There were a large number of attempted strikes that were either foiled, through diligent efforts of law enforcement and military, or failed due to technical issues and poor execution.

Our new reality is that the world faces terrorist attacks every day from either domestic, homegrown violent extremists, or international terrorists. The purpose, as security professionals, is to safeguard the people, property, and places that the service is hired to protect. This lesson is broken into four major sections: Government Agency Overview, International Terrorism, Domestic Terrorism/Homegrown Violent Extremism, and Defense Strategies.

The criminal acts perpetrated on September 11, 2001 forced national and international agencies to redefine terrorism and reanalyze terrorist strategies. To this day, the definition continues to shift to match the actions taken by groups who wish to commit acts of terror. Every security post has different attack vectors. Depending upon the venue, the client, and the material under protection, the post may attract the attention of different terrorist groups. For this reason, it is important to understand the largest and most active terrorist groups, the methods and goals. With this understanding, steps can be taken to harden post defenses. Awareness is always the first line of defense.

Government Agency Overview

U.S. Department of Homeland Security

In response to the terrorist attacks of September 11, 2001, the Department of Homeland Security (DHS) was created through the integration of all or part of 22 different Federal departments and agencies into a unified, integrated Department. The goal was to combine a hodge-podge of government agencies with different reporting structures into a single organization with broad information sharing. The primary goal of the department is protecting the United States and its citizens.

As of June 2016, the DHS included the following operational and support components:
- Directorate for Management
- Domestic Nuclear Detection Office
- Federal Emergency Management Agency (FEMA)
- Federal Law Enforcement Training Center (FLETC)
- National Protection and Programs Directorate
- Office of Health Affairs
- Office of Intelligence and Analysis

- Office of Operations Coordination
- Office of Policy
- Science and Technology Directorate
- Transportation Security Administration (TSA)
- United States Citizenship and Immigration Services (USCIS)
- United States Coast Guard (USCG)
- United States Customs and Border Protection (CBP)
- United States Immigration and Customs Enforcement (ICE)
- United States Secret Service (USSS)

There are five homeland security missions:
1. Prevent terrorism and enhancing security.
2. Secure and manage our borders.
3. Enforce and administer our immigration laws.
4. Safeguard and secure cyberspace.
5. Ensure resilience to disasters.

The DHS has authority to work both inside and outside the US borders. It is the 3rd largest government department behind the Department of Veterans Affairs and Department of Defense.

Source: *Department of Homeland Security*, https://www.dhs.gov

Federal Bureau of Investigation (FBI), Counterterrorism Division (CTD)

The CTD division of the FBI investigates and disrupts terrorist activities within the US borders (Operations Branch II), plus tracks and maintains a global database of international terrorists and terrorist organizations (Operations Branch I).

The National Joint Terrorism Task Force (NJTTF) falls under the CTD.

National Joint Terrorism Task Force (NJTTF)

"The National Joint Terrorism Task Force, or NJTTF, was established in 2002 to manage the burgeoning Joint Terrorism Task Force program—the number of task forces almost doubled overnight, from 35 pre-9/11 to… [over 100] after 9/11. Of course, JTTFs have been around since the 1980s, starting in New York and Chicago. Originally located at FBI Headquarters, the NJTTF moved to the multi-agency National Counterterrorism Center (NCTC), where it performs its mission while also working with NCTC personnel to exchange information, analyze data, and plan anti-terrorism strategies."[1]

The NJTTF is led and funded by the FBI with participation from 55 other federal agencies plus over 500 state agencies and local enforcement.

National Incident Management System (NIMS)

"The National Incident Management System (NIMS) provides a systematic, proactive approach to guide departments and agencies at all levels of government, nongovernmental organizations, and the private sector to work seamlessly to prevent, protect against, respond to, recover from, and mitigate the effects of incidents, regardless of cause, size, location, or complexity, in order to reduce the loss of life and property and harm to the environment. NIMS works hand in hand with the National Response Framework (NRF). NIMS provides the template for the management of incidents, while the NRF provides the structure and mechanisms for national-level policy for incident management…"

"NIMS is not an operational incident management or resource allocation plan. NIMS represents a core set of doctrines, concepts, principles, terminology, and organizational processes that enables effective, efficient, and collaborative incident management…"

---

1   Federal Bureau of Investigation. https://www.fbi.gov/investigate/terrorism

"This framework forms the basis for interoperability and compatibility that will, in turn, enable a diverse set of public and private organizations to conduct well-integrated and effective emergency management and incident response operations. Emergency management is the coordination and integration of all activities necessary to build, sustain, and improve the capability to prepare for, protect against, respond to, recover from, or mitigate against threatened or actual natural disasters, acts of terrorism, or other manmade disasters. It does this through a core set of concepts, principles, procedures, organizational processes, terminology, and standard requirements applicable to a broad community of NIMS users."[2]

---

2   National Incident Management System. 2008. U.S. Department of Homeland Security. Washington, D.C.

International Terrorism

United States Code, 2009 Edition, Title 18 - Crimes and Criminal Procedure, Part 1, - Crimes, Chapter 113B – Terrorism

§ 2331 – Definitions

(1) the term "international terrorism" means activities that—

    (A) involve violent acts or acts dangerous to human life that are a violation of the criminal laws of the United States or of any State, or that would be a criminal violation if committed within the jurisdiction of the United States or of any State;

    (B) appear to be intended—

        (i)   to intimidate or coerce a civilian population;

        (ii) to influence the policy of a government by intimidation or coercion; or

        (iii) to affect the conduct of a government by mass destruction, assassination, or kidnapping; and

    (C) occur primarily outside the territorial jurisdiction of the United

States, or transcend national boundaries in terms of the means by which they are accomplished, the persons they appear intended to intimidate or coerce, or the locale in which their perpetrators operate or seek asylum;

§2332b. Acts of terrorism transcending national boundaries

(a) Prohibited Acts. –

    (1) Offenses. – Whoever, involving conduct transcending national boundaries and in a circumstance described in subsection (b) –

        (A) kills, kidnaps, maims, commits an assault resulting in serious bodily injury, or assaults with a dangerous weapon any person within the United States; or

        (B) creates a substantial risk of serious bodily injury to any other person by destroying or damaging any structure, conveyance, or other real or personal property within the United States or by attempting or conspiring to destroy or damage any structure, conveyance, or other real or personal property within the United States;

    in violation of the laws of any State, or the United States, shall be punished as prescribed in subsection (c).

    (2) Treatment of threats, attempts and conspiracies. – Whoever threatens to commit an offense under paragraph (1), or attempts or conspires to do so, shall be punished under subsection (c).

(f) Investigative Authority. –

In addition to any other investigative authority with respect to violations of this title, the Attorney General shall have primary investigative responsibility for all Federal crimes of terrorism, and any violation of section 351(e), 844(e), 844(f)(1), 956(b), 1361, 1366(b), 1366(c), 1751(e), 2152, or 2156 of this title, and the Secretary of the Treasury shall assist the Attorney General at the request of the Attorney General. Nothing in this section shall be construed to interfere with the authority of the United States Secret Service under section 3056.

Overview

The key aspect to defining international terrorism is, "occur primarily outside the territorial jurisdiction of the United States, or transcend

national boundaries in terms of the means by which they are
accomplished." Governmental agencies and the military have spent a
significant effort hardening the US borders and US facilities outside
its borders, making them difficult to attack. Therefore, the terrorists
have shifted their focus to soft targets such as hotels, restaurants
and other businesses owned by US interests. They have also attacked
public transportation (trains and airplanes) and public gatherings both
inside and outside of the US. For example, in 2009 Umar Farouk "the
Underwear Bomber" Abdul Mutallab, trained by Al Qaeda, attempted
to detonate a bomb on Northwest Airlines Flight 253 and in 2010 Faisal
Shahzad, trained by the Pakistani Taliban, attempted to detonate a car
bomb in Times Square during New Year's Eve celebrations.

Today, the primary driving forces behind terrorism are religion and
ethnicity. "The post-Cold War period witnessed a resurgence of ethnicity
and religiosity. As a result, groups driven by ethnicity and religion now
account for about 70-80 percent of all terrorist groups. Furthermore, the
ethnonationalist and religious groups have the greatest staying power."[1]

Tools

The preferred tool of the terrorist is the explosive, which accounts
for more than 70% of attacks. "Terrorist groups obtain factory-
manufactured explosives through theft or from a terrorist state
sponsor...Terrorist recruits can master bomb-manufacturing skills in a
short period of time, and knowledge of how to handle and manufacture
explosives and explosive devices is widely available on the Internet
and in *The Terrorist Handbook*."[2] Security should be aware of the type
of products held in storage in the facilities they protect. A seemingly
innocent chemical or compound with legitimate everyday use may be
used as a component of explosives. Thefts, especially of large quantities
of a single element, must be treated seriously and reported to authorities.
Even purchases of unusual quantities of some compounds should be
treated with suspicion, especially if paid for with cash.

---

1   Steven, G., & Gunaratna, R. (2004). *Counterterrorism*. Santa Barbara, CA: ABC-
    CLIO, Inc. p.11.
2   Steven, G., & Gunaratna, R. (2004). *Counterterrorism*. Santa Barbara, CA: ABC-
    CLIO, Inc. p.50.

Unless a suicide attack, the most common explosive implementation is to place a bomb and leave it on a timer or remote detonator. Later, at a time designated to have the greatest effect, the bomb is detonated. This is why security teams must be vigilant and always aware of bags, luggage, containers or vehicles left unattended in unexpected areas. Terrorists often place multiple bombs and rig them to detonate simultaneously to increase damage and cover potential malfunctions. Furthermore, some bombs will be set to detonate at different times. The later detonations are targeted at first responders. The goal is not only inflict damage upon the intended target, but those law enforcement, fire, and medical services who arrive later to help the wounded. For example, the February 26, 1993 World Trade Center bombing had a secondary cyanide-gas chemical bomb targeted at first responders that failed to detonate.

The secondary tool of choice is conventional firearms. Unlike most bomb attacks, firearm attacks must be carried out in person. These persons will kill as many people as possible until they are eliminated by responders. It is rare for a shooter to surrender to authorities or attempt escape. Terrorists will sometimes carry explosives and attempt to end their attack with a suicide bomb.

An additional tool used recently by terrorists is a vehicle. These individuals purposefully drive the vehicle into large crowds in the attempt to kill and maim large number of victims.

Tactics

International terrorist groups are often well-funded, well equipped, and have highly trained. Events are researched and planned months ahead of time. Significant effort is placed behind crafting tactics and strategy. Locations are surveilled and plans rehearsed. Once execution starts, there is no deviation from the plan. Security should be extremely suspicious of anyone appearing to test security responses and times, taking photos of and notes on facilities, access ways, entrances, and of security operations.

The Prime goals of international terrorism groups are to instill fear, disrupt livelihoods, and disrupt the economy of targeted groups. These goals cannot be achieved with isolated, local events. Therefore, international terrorists focus on large scale events that will send shockwaves through entire regions. Targets include infrastructure such as water, power; especially nuclear facilities, oil and natural gas pipelines. The groups attempt to disrupt financial centers such as the World Trade Center, stock exchanges, or Federal Reserve Banks. Other high-value targets are airports, train depots, and shipping ports. For example, the Port of Los Angeles handles nearly $1.2 billion worth of cargo daily, is the 18th largest port in the world and the largest port in the United States. The Port of Long Beach, a few miles down the coast from the Port of Los Angeles, is the 20th largest port in the world and the second largest port in the United States. Other at-risk venues hold symbolic value and have large crowds of people. These are places such as Disney Land/World and other amusement parks, Fourth of July celebrations, New Year's celebrations, large sporting events such as the Super Bowl, World Series baseball games, or World Cup games as examples.

Chemical, Biological, Radiological and Nuclear Attack (CBRN)

Chemical

Chemical agents is a category of broad spectrum of man-made toxins that are designed to incapacitate, harm, main or kill those who come into contact with them. They range from "less-than-lethal" tear gases used by police and military to disperse crowds to deadly vapors such as sarin or chlorine gas.

The French were the first to use chemical weapons in combat in 1914 during World War I. The chemical agents used ranged from disabling agents such as tear gas up to fully lethal chemicals such as chlorine gas. The agents were used in an attempt to unseat entrenched soldiers and capture or reclaim territory.

After World War I, the Geneva Protocol, signed in 1925, outlawed the use of lethal chemical weapons. However, some nations still used lethal chemical agents in conflict. For example, in the Iran-Iraq war of 1980-1988, Iraq used lethal chemical agents against Iran and Iraqi Kurds

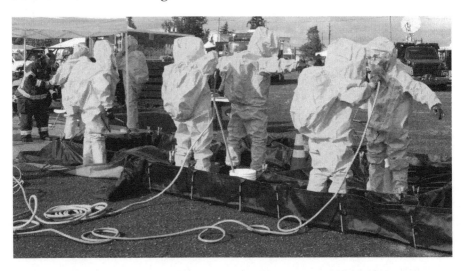

resulting in an estimated 20,000 deaths. During the Syrian Civil War (2013-) the Syrian government has been accused of at least three (3) separate chemical attacks. An independent United Nations investigation confirmed the use of rockets to deliver sarin nerve agent civilians. There were an estimated 280 to 1,700 deaths from the attacks.

Less-than-lethal chemical agents are still used worldwide by military and law enforcement to suppress riots, disperse crowds and flush out entrenched suspects.

Deadly chemical agents are notoriously difficult to deploy and can affect the users as well as the intended targets with a mere shift of the wind. Many terrorist groups (domestic and international) have attempted to deploy chemical agents without success. With one exception, only militaries have successfully deployed chemical agents against targets. The notable exception was in 1995 when the Japanese domestic terrorist group Aum Shinrikyo successfully deployed sarin on the Tokyo subway. 12 passengers were killed, 50 seriously injured and over 5,000 were temporarily blinded.

However, that has not stopped terrorist groups from planning and attempting to use chemical agents. "Analysis of an al-Qa'ida document recovered in Afghanistan in summer 2002 indicates the group has crude procedures for making mustard agent, sarin, and VX…Training videos found in Afghanistan show al-Qa'ida tests of easily produced chemical agents based on cyanide."[3]

Biological

"Biological weapons [(BW)] are weapons that achieve their intended effects by infecting people with disease-causing microorganisms and other replicative entities, including viruses, infectious nucleic acids and prions. The chief characteristic of biological agents is their ability to multiply in a host over time. The disease they may cause is the result of the interaction between the biological agent, the host (including the host's genetic constitution, nutritional status and the immunological status of the host's population) and the environment (e.g., sanitation, temperature, water quality, population density)."[4] The United Nations signed a "multilateral disarmament treaty banning the development, production and stockpiling of an entire category of weapons of mass destruction... The [Biological Weapons Convention] (BWC) entered into force on 26 March 1975."[5]

---

3   Central Intelligence Agency. *Terrorist CBRN: Materials and Effects*. Retrieved from the web https://www.cia.gov/library/reports/general-reports-1/terrorist_cbrn/ terrorist_CBRN.htm

4   The Centre for Excellence in Emergency Preparedness. *What is CBRN?* Ontario, Canada. http://www.ceep.ca/

5   United Nations Office for Disarmament Affairs. Biological Weapons. https://www. un.org/disarmament/wmd/bio/

Biological weapons have been used for thousands of years. Some of the first recorded instances are of the Romans using catapults to launch rotted carcasses over walls into besieged cities to spread disease. In US history, blankets used to cover smallpox victims were later given to "hostile" Native American tribes to spread the disease among the tribes. In 2001, weaponized anthrax was mailed to several news outlets and US Senators resulting in five (5) deaths and seventeen (17) other infections.

There is great concern about the accidental or deliberate release of biological agents considered "extinct" in the general population. This could have a profound and immense deadly impact since there is currently no natural resistance to these diseases in modern populations. These diseases are extremely rare or at undetectable levels in the world population, but still exist in research labs around the world and held by various governments. Example diseases are smallpox where vaccine is no longer administered. The disease killed an estimated 300–500 million people in the 20th century alone and the H1N1 influenza virus (which killed 500 million people worldwide between 1918 and 1920). In 2015, as part of the development of field test for biological weapons, the US Department of Defense accidentally shipped live samples of anthrax around the country to fifty (50) research facilities and three (3) foreign research facilities. The shipment was supposed to contain dead or inactive spores. "In 1947 the Soviet Union established a smallpox weapons factory in the city of Zagorsk, 75 km to the northeast of Moscow. An outbreak of weaponized smallpox occurred during testing at a facility on an island in the Aral Sea in 1971... In March 2004 smallpox scabs were found inside an envelope in a book on Civil War medicine in Santa Fe, New Mexico...In July 2014 several vials of smallpox were discovered in an FDA laboratory at the National Institutes of Health location in Bethesda, Maryland."[6]

"Spray devices disseminating biological warfare (BW) agents have the highest potential impact. Both 11 September attack leader Mohammad Atta and Zacharias Moussaoui expressed interest in crop dusters, raising...concern that al-Qa'ida has considered using aircraft to disseminate BW agents."[7]

---

6   Wikipedia. *Smallpox*. https://en.wikipedia.org/wiki/Smallpox
7   Central Intelligence Agency. Terrorist CBRN: Materials and Effects. Retrieved from

Radiological

Radiological bombs are also called "Dirty Bombs" or "Radiological Dispersal Devices" (RDD). These devices "combine conventional explosives with strontium, cesium, or some other highly radioactive isotope. These substances are used in cancer radiotherapy, the search for oil deposits, sterilization of food, etc. Sadly, throwaway quantities have been found."[8]

The potential impact of a RDD varies depending upon the source. Media reports suggest affected areas remain contaminated and unusable for years while most technical experts suggest the harmful effects last only a few days. Most experts suggest that few actual immediate deaths would result from a RDD, but the emotional impact from fear and concern would have the greatest impact. "Most RDDs would not release enough radiation to kill people or cause severe illness - the conventional explosive itself would be more harmful to individuals than the radioactive material. However, depending on the situation, an RDD explosion could create fear and panic, contaminate property, and require potentially costly

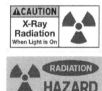

---

the web https://www.cia.gov/

8   Hattersley, J.G. (2005 January). Of Dirty Bombs and the Health Benefits of Low-Level Radiation and Toxins. *Townsend Letter for Doctors and Patients.*

cleanup. Making prompt, accurate information available to the public may prevent the panic sought by terrorists."[9]

Nuclear

The threat of a nuclear terrorist attack comes in two forms: sabotage of a nuclear reactor and detonation of an improvised nuclear device (IND).

After the terrorist plane attacks of September 11, 2001 all nuclear facilities in the United States and Europe were hardened against air strikes. Most nuclear facilities in Europe were even outfitted with anti-aircraft defensive weapons. Additional protections were also added for the transport and storage of spent nuclear fuel and other high activity shipments.

"An [Improvised Nuclear Device] (IND) is intended to cause a yield-producing nuclear explosion. An IND could consist of diverted nuclear weapon components, a modified nuclear weapon, or indigenous-designed device."[10] The international terrorist group al-Qa'ida has been barefaced

9   U.S. Nuclear Regulatory Commission. (2012 December). *Fact Sheet on Dirty Bombs*.
      https://www.nrc.gov/reading-rm/doc-collections/fact-sheets/fs-dirty-bombs.html
10   U.S. Nuclear Regulatory Commission. Terrorist CBRN: Materials and Effects.
      https://www.cia.gov/library/reports/general-reports-1/terrorist_cbrn/terrorist_
      CBRN.htm

about their desire and attempts to acquire fissile material to develop an IND.

There is great concern over black market sale of nuclear materials by international organized crime, especially from the former Soviet republic Moldova. "In October 2015, it was reported that Moldovan authorities working with the FBI have stopped four attempts from 2010 to 2015 by gangs with suspected connections to Russia's intelligence services that sought to sell radioactive material to ISIS and other Middle Eastern extremists."[11]

---

11   Wikipedia. *Nuclear terrorism*. https://en.wikipedia.org/wiki/Nuclear_terrorism

Domestic Terrorism/ Homegrown Violent Extremism

The focus of this section is not on international terrorism, or those actions taken by organizations outside the US borders, but those taken by US Citizens against their own countrymen. Terrorist actions taken by citizens against other citizens is commonly known as Domestic Terrorism.

The threat posed by domestic terrorists/homegrown violent extremists is far greater than international terrorists for those within living and working within US borders. Furthermore, right-wing extremists perpetrate more domestic attacks than Islamic extremists. "Law enforcement agencies reported they were more concerned about the activities of right-wing extremist groups than Islamic extremists in their jurisdictions (about 74 percent versus 39 percent) due to the 'menacing' rhetoric used by some of these groups — and that they were training officers to take caution when they saw signs of potentially violent individuals...

"Pilgrim said he found it offensive that, after Sept. 11, some Americans bemoaned that terrorism had finally breached U.S. borders."

"'That is ignoring and trivializing — if not just summarily dismissing — all the people, especially the peoples of color in this country, who were lynched in this country; who had their homes bombed in this country; who were victims of race riots,' he said evoking lynching victims who were often burned, castrated, shot, stabbed — and in some cases beheaded."[1]

United States Code, 2009 Edition, Title 18 - Crimes and Criminal Procedure, Part 1, - Crimes, Chapter 113B – Terrorism[2]

§ 2331 – Definitions

(5) the term "domestic terrorism" means activities that—
  (A) involve acts dangerous to human life that are a violation of the criminal laws of the United States or of any State;
  (B) appear to be intended—
    (i) to intimidate or coerce a civilian population;
    (ii) to influence the policy of a government by intimidation or coercion; or
    (iii) to affect the conduct of a government by mass destruction, assassination, or kidnapping; and
  (C) occur primarily within the territorial jurisdiction of the United States.

As part of the ever-shifting nature of terrorism, the Department of Homeland Security (DHS) no longer refers to just Domestic Terrorism. Rather, in a July 20, 2015 update to their website, the DHS now places these actions under the broader category of "Homegrown Violent Extremism" (HVE).

"Violent extremists are defined as 'individuals who support or commit

1 Craven, J. (2015 June 24). White Supremacists More Dangerous To America Than Foreign Terrorists, Study Says. The Huffington Post. http://www.huffingtonpost.com

2 U.S. Government Publishing Office. https://www.gpo.gov

ideologically-motivated violence to further political goals.' Violent Extremist threats within the United States can come from a range of violent extremist groups and individuals, including Domestic Terrorists and Homegrown Violent Extremists (HVEs). DHS defines Domestic Terrorism as: Any act of violence that is dangerous to human life or potentially destructive of critical infrastructure or key resources committed by a group or individual based and operating entirely within the United States or its territories without direction or inspiration from a foreign terrorist group. The act is a violation of the criminal laws of the United States or of any state or other subdivision of the United States and appears to be intended to intimidate or coerce a civilian population, to influence the policy of a government by intimidation or coercion, or to affect the conduct of a government by mass destruction, assassination, or kidnapping. A domestic terrorist differs from a homegrown violent extremist in that the former is not inspired by, and does not take direction from, a foreign terrorist group or other foreign power. DHS defines a HVE as: A person of any citizenship who has lived or operated primarily in the United States or its territories who advocates, is engaged in, or is preparing to engage in ideologically-motivated terrorist activities (including providing material support to terrorism) in furtherance of political or social objectives promoted by a terrorist organization, but who is acting independently of direction by a terrorist organization.

"The threat posed by violent extremism is neither constrained by international borders nor limited to any single ideology. Groups and individuals inspired by a range of personal, religious, political, or other ideological beliefs promote and use violence. Increasingly sophisticated use of the Internet, social media, and information technology by violent extremists adds an additional layer of complexity. Accordingly, DHS has designed a countering violent extremism (CVE) approach that addresses all forms of violent extremism, regardless of ideology, and that focuses not on radical thought or speech but instead on preventing violent attacks. This approach provides numerous physical and virtual environments to promote information sharing and collaboration between Federal, State, Local, Territorial, Tribal, Private, Civilian, and International entities working to counter the threat of violent extremism."[3]

---

3   Department of Homeland Security. Retrieved from the web on October 1, 2015.
     http://www.dhs.gov/topic/countering-violent-extremism

For an act to be considered terrorism it must include at least one of the following:

- "Violence or the threat of violence;
- "Calculated to create fear and alarm;
- "Intended to coerce certain actions;
- "Motive must include a political objective;
- "Generally directed against civilian targets; and
- "It can be a group or an individual."[4]

From 2001–2009 the most common attack used in domestic terrorism was arson (46%). Fortunately, most domestic terror attacks result in no fatalities. Bombings represented 18.7% of domestic attacks and armed attacks represented 7.7%, which account for nearly all fatalities.[5]

Many hate groups fall into the category of HVEs due to their tactics, violence, and political motives. Although every state has documented hate groups, Texas has the most with 84, followed by California with 68, and Florida with 58. Our nation's capital, Washington, D.C., has 18 documented hate groups.[6]

The subject of domestic terrorism/homegrown violent extremists is broad, deep, and highly complex. This section provides an overview of the threat posed by HVEs, a brief discussion of the most prevalent HVE groups, common tactics and tools, and example events. The purpose is general education and understanding with the goal of early identification and threat avoidance. It is not intended as a comprehensive analysis of all HVE groups or events.

Eco-terrorists and Animal Rights Extremists

4   Bruce Hoffman, *Inside Terrorism* (New York, N.Y.: Columbia University Press, 2006), pp. 40–41.

5   Muhlhausen, D.B., & McNeill, J.B. Terror Trends 40 Years' Data on International and Domestic Terrorism. (Washington, D.C.: The Heritage Foundation, 2011), pp. 9-10.

6   Southern Poverty Law Center. 2016. The Hate Map. Retrieved from the web on September 19, 2016. https://www.splcenter.org/hate-map

Sometimes known as "Radical Environmentalist and Animal Rights" (REAR), eco-terrorists and animal rights extremists focus their efforts on destroying businesses and universities that support or conduct animal testing and research, forestry, furriers, hunters, and land development. These groups have vandalized or destroyed hundreds of millions of dollars' worth of property and research. The cell operates as individuals or small-group "leaderless" cells. The primary tool of eco-terrorist groups is arson.

Although animal welfare groups date back to the 1800s in the United Kingdom and the United States, eco-terrorists and animal rights extremism took hold in the United States during the 1970s. Their goals are to inflict economic harm by disrupting operations and destroying physical and intellectual property. In past decades care was taken not to harm "any animal, human and nonhuman" by their actions. However, in recent years the group rhetoric has shifted to direct threatening of researchers, food producers, and law enforcement. Although no assassinations have yet taken place on United States soil, European scientists, researchers and business executives have been killed for their work by eco-terrorist and anarchist groups. With the shift to public threats of violence against people, there is growing concern that there may be similar attacks here in the US. A 2003 bombing in Pleasanton, California was claimed by the previously unknown group named "Revolutionary Cells of the Animal Liberation Brigade." A note claiming responsibility for the bombing included, "Now you will all reap what you have sown. All customers and their families are considered legitimate targets… You never know when your house, your car even, might go boom… Or maybe it will be a shot in the dark… We will now be doubling the size of every device we make. Today it is 10 pounds, tomorrow 20… until your buildings are nothing more than rubble. It is time for this war to truly have two sides. No more will all the killing be done by the oppressors, now the oppressed will strike back."

In 2008, the Federal Bureau of Investigation (FBI) identified eco-terrorists and animal rights extremists as a significant domestic threat. "Together, eco-terrorists and animal rights extremists are one of the most serious domestic terrorism threats in the U.S. today, for several good reasons:

- "The sheer volume of their crimes (over 2,000 since 1979);
- "The huge economic impact (losses of more than $110 million since 1979);
- "The wide range of victims (from international corporations to lumber companies to animal testing facilities to genetic research firms); and
- "Their increasingly violent rhetoric and tactics (one recent communiqué sent to a California product testing company said: 'You might be able to protect your buildings, but can you protect the homes of every employee?')."[7]

"Since the mid-1980s, California has been unequalled in the number of incidents claimed by [Animal Liberation Front] ALF and other groups. Altogether, approximately 54% of all documented incidents occurred in the western United States (excluding Hawaii)."[8]

The most destructive tool used by eco-terrorists and animal rights extremists is arson. Improvised incendiary devices with time mechanisms are common, with build instructions found on Animal Liberation Front (ALF) and Earth Liberation Front (ELF) websites. These criminals surveille targets beforehand and plan strikes. There is often tremendous effort made in researching targets including photographic and video surveillance, security details, employee movements, Internet research and even review of trade industry publications.

Animal Enterprise Protection Act of 1992 (AETA)

Commonly known as the "Animal Enterprise Terrorism Act" (AETA), this federal law makes it a crime to "[damage] or [interfere] with the operations of an animal enterprise."[9] Actually committing the act, attempting to commit the act, and/or conspiring to commit the act all share equal penalties. The penalties of restitution, fines, jail and prison are on a sliding scale based upon the dollar value of the damage caused

---

7   Putting Intel to Work: Against ELF and ALF Terrorists. Retrieved from the web on September 18, 2016. https://archives.fbi.gov/archives/news/stories/2008/june/ecoterror_063008

8   The Animal Enterprise Protection Act of 1992 and Mandated Report. September 2, 1993. U.S. Department of Justice

9   18 U.S. Code § 43 - Force, violence, and threats involving animal enterprises

or any deaths that result from the acts. In 2006, the Act was amended to increase the penalties and provide better protection of individuals targeted by eco-terrorists and animal rights extremists.

The law was first used in 1998 against Peter Young and Justin Samuel. There have been more than 30 indictments of individuals since 2006 under the AETA.

Operation Backfire

Led by the FBI, "Operation Backfire" is a multi-agency criminal investigation task force whose focus is domestic eco-terrorism.

Animal Liberation Front (ALF)

Originating in the United Kingdom in the mid-1970s, The Animal Liberation Front (ALF) is considered one of the most active extremist groups in the United States. The US branch first saw operations in the late 1970s.

ALF operates as leaderless cells and maintains no formal membership lists. According to postings, membership is achieved by "direct action" to halt the abuse and exploitation of animals. "Direct action" is seen as destruction of, or economic harm to, animal research facilities. A guiding principle of the organization is avoid acts that harm "any animal, human and nonhuman." It has generally held to this guideline. Criminal activities by AFL against furriers, restaurants, animal research companies, and universities have increased over the years.

"Before it established a press office in the U.S., ALF activities were frequently publicized by People for the Ethical Treatment of Animals (PETA), a Norfolk, Virginia-based animal rights organization whose controversial advertisement campaigns have generated substantial publicity since the group's founding in 1980. PETA has openly supported ALF: in 1995, the organization gave $45,200 to the legal defense of Rod Coronado, while co-founder Ingrid Newkirk applauds ALF's efforts in two of her books."[10]

---

10   Anti-Defamation League. *Ecoterrorism: Extremism in the Animal Rights and Environmentalist Movements*. Retrieved from the web on September 19, 2016. http://

Common ALF slogans:
- Meat is murder
- Animal Auschwitz
- Meat is death and you are next
- Liberation is love

Earth Liberation Front (ELF)

Before a discussion of the Earth Liberation Front (ELF) can begin, it is important to understand the group's progenitor organization, Earth First!.

Earth First! was founded in 1979 by Dave Foreman, Mike Roselle, Howie Wolke, Bart Koehler, and Ron Kezar. Predominantly associated with anti-logging and protection of trees, the group was the first to organize tree sit-ins and "tree spiking", the insertion of metal or ceramic spikes in trees in an effort to damage saws, as a tactic to thwart logging. The group also actively resisted road construction and damn building.

In 1989 a group of Earth First! members sabotaged a high-speed desert motorcycle race by blocking a darkened tunnel with railroad ties. If the race coordinators had not discovered the blockage before the start, it could have killed many racers.

In 1991, co-founder Dave Foreman pled guilty to conspiracy to destroy electrical lines leading to an Arizona nuclear power plant.

Co-founder Mike Roselle registered the Earth First! Action Fund as a California business in 1990. In the early 1990s, Earth First! leadership claimed to abandon all illegal actions.

The group publishes the "Earth First! Journal." This journal often contains highly inflammatory rhetoric. A September 1989 edition contained the line "A 'Hit List' is available upon discreet inquiry."[11] An April 1996 edition of the publications included "Eco-F*cker Hit List" which included the California Forestry Association and Oil Industry

archive.adl.org/learn/ext_us/ecoterrorism.html

11 Activist Facts, Center for Organizational Research and Education. Retrieved from the web on September 26, 2016 https://www.activistfacts.com/organizations/271-earth-first/

Public Relation Executives. "The 20th Anniversary issue of the Journal noted: 'Trees are for hanging. Kill a developer.' …Dave Foreman's words: 'The blood of timber executives is my natural drink, and the wail of dying forest supervisors is music to my ears.'"[12]

"In 1992, the ELF was founded in Brighton, England, by Earth First! members who refused to abandon criminal acts as a tactic when others wished to mainstream Earth First! In 1993, the ELF was listed for the first time along with the ALF in a communique declaring solidarity in actions between the two groups. This unity continues today with a crossover of leadership and membership. It is not uncommon for the ALF and the ELF to post joint declarations of responsibility for criminal actions on their web-sites. In 1994, founders of the San Francisco branch of Earth First! published in The Earth First! Journal a recommendation that Earth First! mainstream itself in the United States, leaving criminal acts other than unlawful protests to the ELF."[13]

"The ELF advocates 'monkeywrenching,' a euphemism for acts of sabotage and property destruction against industries and other entities perceived to be damaging to the natural environment. 'Monkeywrenching' includes tree spiking, arson, sabotage of logging or construction equipment, and other types of property destruction. Speeches given by Jonathan Paul and Craig Rosebraugh at the 1998 National Animal Rights Conference held at the University of Oregon, promoted the unity of both the ELF and the ALF movements. The ELF posted information on the ALF website until it began its own website in January 2001, and is listed in the same underground activist publications as the ALF."[14]

Theodore "the Unabomber" Kaczynski
Theodore "the Unabomber" Kaczynski was an avid supporter of

---

12 Activist Facts, Center for Organizational Research and Education. Retrieved from the web on September 26, 2016 https://www.activistfacts.com/organizations/271-earth-first/

13 United States. Cong. House. House Resources Committee, Subcommittee on Forests and Forest Health. Hearings, Feb. 12, 2002. Washington: GPO, 2002. FBI. gov. Web. 30 September 2016.

14 United States. Cong. House. House Resources Committee, Subcommittee on Forests and Forest Health. Hearings, Feb. 12, 2002. Washington: GPO, 2002. FBI. gov. Web. 30 September 2016.

and follower of Earth First! His cabin contained many Earth First! publications and many of his victims were also on the groups published "hit lists." The FBI believes that Kaczynski attended at least one Earth First! event.

Sovereign Citizen

Starting in the 1970s, the sovereign citizen movement is a group of tax protesters, financial-scheme promoters, and often commit white-collar crime. Members of the movement believe that although they are citizens of and live within the borders of the United States, they are separate from the United States. They reject their US citizenship and assert only their common-law state citizenship. Some may recognize state laws, but all refuse to recognize the federal government, federal laws or the authority of federal courts. They refuse to pay taxes.

Some of the more organized groups hold false courts and issue warrants or death sentences for judges and law enforcement officers and file frivolous lawsuits against public officials. Law enforcement officers across the country have been shot and killed during traffic stops initiated for lack of valid license plates or registration tags.

According to a 2010 FBI report,[15] common crimes committed by sovereign citizens include:

- Check fraud
- Murder and physical assault
- Impersonate law enforcement
- Threaten judges, law enforcement and government personnel
- Create, use and distribute fake money, passports, license plates and driver's licenses
- Mortgage fraud, bank fraud, insurance fraud and "redemption" schemes
- Money laundering
- Tax evasion
- Weapons charges

15 Domestic Terrorism: The Sovereign Citizen Movement. FBI Retrieved from the web on October 1, 2016. https://archives.fbi.gov/archives/news/stories/2010/april/sovereigncitizens_041310

"[A] 2014 report by the National Consortium for the Study of Terrorism and Responses to Terrorism, a survey of law-enforcement officials and agencies across the United States concluded that the [Sovereign Citizen] movement was the single greatest threat to their communities, ranking above Islamic terrorists and jihadists."[16] According to a Forbes Magazine article, in 2012 there were "an estimated 300,000 people in the movement, and approximately one third of these are what I would call hard-core believers – people willing to act on their beliefs rather than simply walk away."[17]

The Sovereign Citizen is sometimes confused with the Militia Movement. Although similar on the surface, they are distinct movements. Militias are primarily paramilitary and focus on firearms, other weapons and military-style training to defend against "invaders" while sovereign citizens focus on anti-government actions.

April 2014, Nevada

For decades, Cliven Bundy illegally grazed his cattle on Nevada federal land owned by the United States Bureau of Land Management (BLM). Bundy had an ongoing 20-year dispute over grazing rights to the BLM land and in 1993 stopped paying the permit fees. In July 2013, a federal judge ordered Bundy to refrain from trespassing on the federal land. Despite the court order, Bundy continued to graze his cattle on the land. In April 2014, the land was temporarily closed in order for the BLM to collect and remove the trespassing cattle. On April 12, 2014, a group of armed protestors confronted the BLM officials and law enforcement rangers. Rather than risk a gun battle, the BLM director ordered the cattle released.

There was some political support for Cliven Bundy from Republican politicians and some conservative personalities. Bundy stated, "I abide by all of Nevada state laws. But I don't recognize the United States government as even existing."[18] Several out of state militia groups and

16   Wikipedia. Retrieved from the web on October 1, 2016. https://en.wikipedia.org/wiki/Sovereign_citizen_movement

17   MacNab, JJ. 13 Feb 2012. What is a Sovereign Citizen? *Forbes Magazine*. Retrieved from the web on October 1, 2016. http://www.forbes.com/sites/jjmacnab/2012/02/13/what-is-a-sovereign-citizen/

18   Ford, Matt. April 14, 2014. The Irony of Cliven Bundy's Unconstitutional Stand.

sovereign citizen groups expressed support for Bundy. Nearly all political support was withdrawn after Bundy made several public statements that were widely considered extremely racist.

By April 18, 2014, it was estimated that nearly 1,500 protestors gathered to support Bundy.

Cliven Bundy was arrested in Portland, OR on February 10, 2016 on multiple federal charges. He was on his way to visit his son at the Malheur National Wildlife Refuge (see *January 2, 2016, Malheur National Wildlife Refuge, OR.*). At least 16 others were charged in association with the 2014 standoff.

As of April 2016, the original uncollected herd has grown to over 1,000 in number and continue to roam the disputed land as untended wild animals.[19]

Lone Offenders/Lone Wolf

Although not new, lone wolf violent extremists are a concerning category of HVEs. According to a 2015 federally funded independent report, the definition of "Lone wolf terrorism is political violence perpetrated by individuals who act alone; who do not belong to an organized terrorist group or network; who act without the direct influence of a leader or hierarchy; and whose tactics and methods are conceived and directed by the individual without any direct outside command or direction."[20] Historically, lone offenders were primarily white supremacists, but in recent years al-Qaeda and ISIL have implemented public relations campaigns using social media, newsletters and magazines to encourage lone offenders to act in the name of radical Islam.

Lone wolf HVE events are broken into two eras: Pre-9/11 and Post-9/11. In the 1990s there were 98 deaths and 305 injured. The primary

---

The Atlantic. http://www.theatlantic.com/

19   Hayden, Jen. April 15, 2016. Deadbeat rancher Cliven Bundy's wild cows are reportedly starving; Nevada and BLM have yet to act. Daily Kos. http://www.dailykos.com

20   Hamm, M.S., Spaaij, R. (2015). *Lone Wolf Terrorism in America: Using Knowledge of Radicalization Pathways to Forge Prevention Strategies.* Indiana State University.

tools used were bombs and the primary targets were women's health facilities and workers. In Post-9/11 as of 2016, the number of deaths is over 120 and injuries are over 200. The primary tools are now firearms and the primary targets are the general populace or specifically hated groups (military, law enforcement, LGBT community, anti-Semitic, etc.).

It is nearly impossible to adequately create a profile of a lone-wolf HVE. Different portraits emerge depending upon the attack motivations. It has been suggested that they have more in common with mass murderers and serial killers than terrorists; the distinction between the two being political motivation.

Oak Creek, Wisconsin, 2012

Army veteran and white supremacist, Wade Page, shot and killed six people and injured four when he opened fire on a Sikh temple as women and children prepared for a communal meal.

Orlando, Florida, 2016

Security guard and Islamic extremist, Omar Mateen, shot and killed 49 people and injured 53 others when he opened fire at a gay nightclub at about 2:00am. Mateen swore allegiance to the Islamic State of Iraq and ISIL in a 9-1-1 call just before the event.

Anarchist Extremism

Anarchist Extremism was imported from Europe to the United States during the late 1880s. The movement is anti-capitalism, anti-globalism, anti-law enforcement and anti-urbanization. Considered far left-wing, each branch of the Anarchist Movement can have a different focus and goals. However, the overarching driver for all members is elimination of all centralized governments and authority.

Anarchist Extremism plagued the presidencies of William McKinley (1897-1901) and Teddy Roosevelt (1901-1909). President McKinley was assassinated by anarchist Leon Czolgosz in September 1901. His vice president, Teddy Roosevelt, took the Office of the President upon his death. During those times and since, the anarchists have conducted bombings and assassinations throughout the country.

Current anarchist movement members are generally peaceful protestors, but there is an extreme element that continues to use violence to deliver messages. Favorite targets for protests and other actions are the Group of Eight (G8) summits, World Trade Organization (WTO) meetings, International Monetary Fund (IMF), World Bank and the World Economic Forum.

Anarchist Extremism continues to be a global terrorist threat, with most of the violent events in Europe. Although activity is seen all over the world, due to the disparate cell structure, events are considered domestic threats and usually handled by local, not federal, law enforcement.

Common Anarchist Slogans:
• No borders, no banks

June 1919, Washington, D.C.

Suicide bomber anarchist Carlo Valdinoc killed himself and the newly appointed Attorney General A. Mitchell Palmer in his home. Other members of government, judges, politicians, law enforcement and industry were the targets of bombings across the country.

January 28, 1975, Washington, D.C and Oakland,

CA

The Weather Underground, an anarchist extremism group, placed bombs at two government buildings: U.S. Agency for International Development in Washington, D.C. and a Department of Defense supply agency in Oakland, CA. Only the bomb at the Washington, D.C. facility detonated, hurting no one, but causing extensive damage.

November 30, 1999, Seattle, Washington

An estimated 40,000 protestors gathered at the Washington State Convention and Trade Center in Seattle, Washington to protest the WTO Ministerial Conference. Commonly called the "N30" or "Battle of Seattle," organized protestors marched down streets from multiple directions and took control of key intersections, causing the cancellation of afternoon WTO sessions. The city sustained millions of dollars in damage from rioting.

Militia Extremism

"A militia is a group of citizens who come together to protect the country, usually during an emergency. Some militia extremists, however, seek to violently attack or overthrow the U.S. government. Often calling themselves 'patriots,' they believe the government has become corrupt, has overstepped its constitutional limits, or has not been able to protect the country against global dangers."[21] These groups believe that the government was subverted by a tyrannical shadow organization which really controls the country, and that members must fortify themselves and train to take back the government and reassert the Constitution. Although not technically part of the Christian Identity/White Supremacy and Sovereign Citizen movements, they often share membership with those in Militia Extremist groups. The militia groups are staunchly survivalist, anti-government, anti-tax, and anti-immigration.

The right-wing, para-military militia extremists have existed in the United States since before World War II. The extremist militia movement began to truly rise in the 1980s and gained significant publicity in the wake of the Oklahoma City bombing in 1995. Although the incident had nothing to do with militias, the media made the erroneous connection which gave

---

21   Militia Extremists. FBI. https://cve.fbi.gov/whatare/?state=domestic

national attention to the movement. The result was an increase in militia membership. By 1996, nearly every state had a militia group, with most having several. Numbers swelled again as the "Y2K" or "Millennium Bug" picked up momentum as many feared the collapse of computers, the economy, the government and Christian religious fervor of the year 2000. Since then, the numbers have been on the decline, with short periods of increased membership and activity.

The right-wing, para-military militia extremists usually target law enforcement, judges, the IRS and government officials. On an increasing basis, they have targeted Muslims and their places of worship.

Posse Comitatus (organization)

Founded in the late 1960s, Posse Comitatus is an extremist organization that crosses into multiple HVE categories including: Militia Extremist, Sovereign Citizen and Christian Identity/White Supremacy.

January 2, 2016, Malheur National Wildlife Refuge, OR

Ammon Bundy, son of Cliven Bundy (see April 2014, Nevada), led a group of armed militia members to take over the Malheur National

Wildlife Refuge in Oregon. Approximately two-dozen took control of a closed federal building on the refuge. Demands from the group included releasing some convicted criminals and releasing federal control of the 1.4-million-acre refuge. Local and federal officers decided to wait them out and blockaded the area, although in the first few weeks the militants were allowed to move freely about. The last militants in the refuge finally surrendered on February 10, 2016. 27 militants were arrested on federal charges for the occupation of the facility.

White Supremacy/Christian Extremism

The White Supremacy movement and Christian Extremism are often intertwined with one supporting the other. Racism through the use of religion promotes violence and religious terrorism to support what is perceived as "God's mandate." Many White Supremacy/Christian Extremism groups recruit new members by attempting to brand themselves as "wholesome" Christian organizations with "family values." The group holds family picnics, bar-b-ques, and other social events. Only later are the true doctrines and abject racism revealed to new members.

In order to garner public support and offset their violent reputation, some white supremacy groups even go so far as to donate money to black churches and other community charities. They promote these public acts to help deny claims of racism and demonstrate their support for the welfare of all citizens. The reality is that these acts are merely a public relations smokescreen and recruitment tool.

In recent years, the white supremacy and Christian extremism groups have capitalized on the immigration and border control controversy as a recruitment tool. They, along with other militia groups, have formed citizen border patrol units along the southern US border with Mexico. They refer to themselves as "Armed Patriots" who seek to keep out illegal immigrants crossing into US territory. The hate groups also claim there is a conspiracy for illegal immigrants to take control of the US Southwest and form the new nation of Aztlan, based upon a counterculture document published in the 1960s.

Political ideologies:
- Anti-race mixing
- Anti-abortion
- Anti-LGBT
- Anti-any non-white race
- Anti-Semitic
- Anti-any non-Christian

Common Slogans:
- White power.
- If it ain't white, it ain't right.

Christian Identity Movement

"Christian Identity is a fervent ideology of racial and religious bigotry that advocates violence, persecution, and conceivably genocide to promote a divine calling to what its followers perceive as a war for the moral character of America as a righteous nation in the balance. Racist hate-groups ranging from the Ku Klux Klan and White Aryan Resistance, militia groups Posse Comitatus and Covenant, the Sword and the Arm of the Lord, and religious groups World Church of the Creator and Worldwide Church of God, base their beliefs on Christian Identity theology."[22] Christian Identity members believe that non-white Christians cannot be saved.

Christian Identity members staunchly "believe that white people are the true Israelites and that Jews and people of color are subhuman 'children of Satan' who, along with the government, are to be destroyed in an apocalyptic battle."[23]

Christian Dominion and Reconstruction Theologies

Christian Dominionism and Dominion Theology are not specific

22 Wong, F.D. MAJ (2011). *Christian Extremism as a Domestic Terror Threat.* (Fort Leavenworth, Kansas: School of Advanced Military Studies United States Army Command and General Staff College, 2011), p. 9.
23 Russell, M.M. MAJ (2002). *Domestic Terrorism: Is America Prepared?* Quantico, VA. United States Marine Corps Command and Staff College.

Christian denominations. Rather, they are beliefs within Protestant denominations. Common beliefs are that Christians are mandated by God to control all religious institutions. Additionally, they are encouraged to dominate politically as part of God's mandate. Advocates are often heard making statements such as "America is a Christian Nation" therefore the bible and "Christian Law" must be the governing law of country. This is despite that the First Amendment to the Constitution of the United States clearly prohibits establishing a State religion, "Congress shall make no law respecting an establishment of religion, or prohibiting the free exercise thereof;"

Christian Reconstructionism is a sub-category of Christian Dominionism. Christian Reconstructionism arose out of conservative Presbyterianism in the early 1970's. Adherents of Christian Reconstructionism believe "that every area dominated by sin must be 'reconstructed' in terms of the Bible."[24]

"The underlying theme of Dominionism and Reconstructionism is the higher calling to do God's will where Biblical law overrules secular law, especially when the secular law is perceived as immoral. It is this belief

---

24 Dominionism and Dominion Theology. Retrieved from the web on November 3, 2015. http://theocracywatch.org/dominionism.htm

that motivates militant anti-abortionists to resort to violence to save innocent, unborn children from an immoral law that sentences them to death."[25]

"One of the key underlying themes of Christian extremism is racism, as Christian Identity ideology advocates violence and justifies bigotry through a religious context. However, the link between Christian extremism and domestic terrorism is not limited to just racist dogmas, but also in the radical interpretation of the Christian call to save the unborn fetus from being murdered through an abortion."[26]

Violence against women's health clinics has existed for decades. Providers have been assassinated, kidnapped, clinics burned, clinics bombed, death threats levied, chemical agents used to disrupt service, plus numerous intimidation and harassment tactics used against patients. It is important for security guards to understand this category of violent extremist as women's health clinics often hire private security to provide protection for the facility, staff, escort patients to and from the parking lot and manage protestors outside clinics. Security guards have been killed in clinic bombings and shootings.

Common Slogans:
- America is a Christian nation.
- Christian law is the only law.

Peckerwood

"In the second half of the 20th century, in prison environments in Texas, California, and possibly elsewhere, the word peckerwood, originally used to refer to white prisoners generally, began to develop a more specific association with members of racist prison gangs and cliques, as well as their associates and hangers-on. This association is strongest in California and Texas, and fairly strong across the West and South in general, but less common in the Midwest and Northeast. In California, the term spread from the prison to the streets in the form of so-called peckerwood

25 Wong, F.D. MAJ (2011). Christian Extremism as a Domestic Terror Threat. (Fort Leavenworth, Kansas: School of Advanced Military Studies United States Army Command and General Staff College, 2011), p. 14.
26 Wong, F.D. MAJ (2011). Christian Extremism as a Domestic Terror Threat. (Fort Leavenworth, Kansas: School of Advanced Military Studies United States Army Command and General Staff College, 2011), p. 33.

gangs, white gangs that mix elements of street gang, prison gang, and racist skinhead gang. Their white supremacy is more often crude than sophisticated and they have a high association with traditional criminal activity, such as drugs. They tend to organize geographically, such as San Fernando Valley Peckerwoods, Inland Empire Peckerwoods, High Desert Peckerwoods, etc.

"Symbolically, the term peckerwood is often represented by various woodpecker images, sometimes in conjunction with other hate symbols. It is also common for white supremacists to use the word itself for a tattoo, or its common shortened version, 'Wood,' as in '100% Wood.' Collectively, peckerwoods in a particular prison or geographic range are often called the 'Woodpile.' Female peckerwoods are referred to as 'featherwoods.'"[27]

Aryan Brotherhood

"The Aryan Brotherhood, a California-based prison gang that was formed in the California prison system during the 1960s."[28] It is has since spread to other states and is especially popular in Texas, with the Aryan Brotherhood of Texas (ABT) being the largest group. It is widely considered one of the most violent white supremacist prison gangs.

Example Incidents

- The Oklahoma City, OK Alfred P. Murrah Federal Building bombing on April 19, 1995 was motivated by the perpetrator's anti-government sentiments, retribution for the siege of the Branch Davidians in Waco, TX (1993), and his Christian extremism. The perpetrator was a U.S. Army veteran and deployed to Kuwait during Operation Desert Storm. He was also known to attended Ku Klux Klan protests.
- The Centennial Olympic Park bombing in Atlanta, GA on July 27, 1996 was motivated by the perpetrator's Christian anti-abortion sentiment. In an April 13, 2005 statement, the perpetrator stated, "…the purpose of the attack on July 27 was to confound, anger and embarrass the Washington government in the eyes of the world for its abominable sanctioning of abortion on demand."

---

27 Peckerwood. Anti-Defamation League. Retrieved from the web on November 4, 2015. http://www.adl.org/combating-hate/hate-on-display/c/peckerwood.html
28 Three Sentenced for Involvement in Aryan Brotherhood of Texas Racketeering Conspiracy. December 9, 2014 FBI. https://www.fbi.gov/

- Abortion clinic bombing in Sandy Springs, GA on January 16, 1997. This was the same perpetrator as the Centennial Olympic Park bombing.
- Abortion clinic bombing in Birmingham, AL on January 29, 1998. This was the same perpetrator as the Centennial Olympic Park bombing.
- Dr. David Gunn was murdered on March 10, 1993 by an anti-abortion activist.
- The Grand Chute, WI Planned Parenthood clinic was bombed on April 1, 2012.

Defense Strategies

The following information is provided by the FBI. "Security guards are trained observers paid to be aware of their surroundings. All of the questions below directly apply to observations made by private security while on duty or not. If any of the observations are made, contact the local supervisor immediately and follow post orders.

This is a message that bears repeating, no matter where you live in the world: Your assistance is needed in preventing terrorist acts.

It's a fact that certain kinds of activities can indicate terrorist plans that are in the works, especially when they occur at or near high profile sites or places where large numbers of people gather—like government buildings, military facilities, utilities, bus or train stations, major public events. If you see or know about suspicious activities, like the ones listed below, please report them immediately to the proper authorities. In the United States, that means your closest Joint Terrorist Task Force, located in an FBI field office. In other countries, that means your closest law enforcement/counterterrorism agency.

Surveillance: Are you aware of anyone video recording or monitoring activities, taking notes, using cameras, maps, binoculars, etc., near key facilities/events?

Suspicious Questioning: Are you aware of anyone attempting to gain information in person, by phone, mail, email, etc., regarding a key facility or people who work there?

Tests of Security: Are you aware of any attempts to penetrate or test physical security or procedures at a key facility/event?

Acquiring Supplies: Are you aware of anyone attempting to improperly acquire explosives, weapons, ammunition, dangerous chemicals, uniforms, badges, flight manuals, access cards or identification for a key facility/event or to legally obtain items under suspicious circumstances that could be used in a terrorist attack?

Suspicious Persons: Are you aware of anyone who does not appear to belong in the workplace, neighborhood, business establishment, or near a key facility/event?

"Dry Runs": Have you observed any behavior that appears to be preparation for a terrorist act, such as mapping out routes, playing out scenarios with other people, monitoring key facilities/events, timing traffic lights or traffic flow, or other suspicious activities?

Deploying Assets: Have you observed abandoned vehicles, stockpiling of suspicious materials, or persons being deployed near a key facility/event?"

Suspicious Behavior

The following list is taken from the "FBI-DHS Private Sector Advisory" poster on identifying suspicious behaviors.

"Businesses can become unwitting participants in illicit or terrorist activities. Be aware of unusual or suspicious purchases or usage of your products and services.

What are common examples?
- Nervous or evasive customer attitudes
- Vague knowledge of product's proper use
- Unusual product quantities
- Refusal to purchase substitutes
- Insistence on in-store pick-up for bulk purchases
- Large cash purchases

How can you help?
- Understand how your products and services may be used illicitly
- Discuss product or service usage with customers and suggest alternatives
- Ask for customer ID and maintain a log of suspicious purchases
- Know your customers and report suspicious activity to authorities

Glossary

Domestic Terrorism: Any act of violence that is dangerous to human life or potentially destructive of critical infrastructure or key resources committed by a group or individual based and operating entirely within the United States or its territories without direction or inspiration from a foreign terrorist group.

Homegrown Violent Extremists (HVEs): A person of any citizenship who has lived or operated primarily in the United States or its territories who advocates, is engaged in, or is preparing to engage in ideologically-motivated terrorist activities (including providing material support to terrorism) in furtherance of political or social objectives promoted by a terrorist organization, but who is acting independently of direction by a terrorist organization.

Sovereign Citizen Movement: Sovereign citizens are anti-government extremists who believe that even though they physically reside in this country, they are separate or "sovereign" from the United States. As a result, they believe they do not have to answer to any government authority, including courts, taxing entities, motor vehicle departments, or law enforcement.

Violent Extremists: Individuals who support or commit

ideologically-motivated violence to further political goals.

Zionist: Refers to the Jewish influence on government and the media industry.

Abbreviations

ABT   Aryan Brotherhood of Texas

AETA   Animal Enterprise Protection Act of 1992

ALF   Animal Liberation Front

BLM   United States Bureau of Land Management

BW   Biological weapon

CIA   Central Intelligence Agency

CNSP   United States Counter Nuclear Smuggling Program

CTD   Counterterrorism Division (of the FBI)

CVE   Countering Violent Extremism

DHS   Department of Homeland Security

ELF   Earth Liberation Front

FBI   Federal Bureau of Investigation

G8   Group of Eight

GICNT Global Initiative to Combat Nuclear Terrorism

HVE   Homegrown Violent Extremist

IMF   International Monetary Fund

IND   Improvised Nuclear Device

LGBT   Lesbian, Gay, Bi-sexual, Transgender

NCTC   National Counterterrorism Center

NIC   National Integration Center

NIMS   National Incident Management System

NJTTF   National Joint Terrorism Task Force

NRF   National Response Framework

RDD   Radiological Dispersal Device

REAR   Radical Environmentalist and Animal Rights

SHAC   Stop Huntingdon Animal Cruelty

WTO   World Trade Organization

References

Activist Facts, Center for Organizational Research and Education. https://www.activistfacts.com/

Age of the Wolf: A Study in the Rise of Lone Wolf and Leaderless Resistance Terrorism. N.A. (2015). Montgomery, AL: *Southern Poverty Law Center.*

Anti-Defamation League. http://www.adl.org/

Bolz, Jr., F., Dudonis, K., & Schulz, D. (2002). *The Counterterrorism Handbook: Tactics, Procedures, and Techniques* (2nd ed.). Boca Raton, FL: CRC Press, LLC.

Central Intelligence Agency. https://www.cia.gov

Centre for Excellence in Emergency Preparedness, The. *What is CBRN?* Ontario, Canada. http://www.ceep.ca/

Craven, J. (2015 June 24). White Supremacists More Dangerous To America Than Foreign Terrorists, Study Says. *The Huffington Post.* http://www.huffingtonpost.com/

Department of Homeland Security. https://www.dhs.gov/

Federal Bureau of Investigation. https://www.fbi.gov

Ford, Matt. (14 Apr 2014). The Irony of Cliven Bundy's Unconstitutional Stand. *The Atlantic.* http://www.theatlantic.com/

Hamm, M.S., Spaaij, R. (2015). *Lone Wolf Terrorism in America: Using Knowledge of Radicalization Pathways to Forge Prevention Strategies.* Indiana State University.

Hattersley, J.G. (2005 January). Of Dirty Bombs and the Health Benefits of Low-Level Radiation and Toxins. *Townsend Letter for Doctors and Patients.*

Hayden, Jen. (15 Apr 2016. Deadbeat rancher Cliven Bundy's wild cows are reportedly starving; Nevada and BLM have yet to act. *Daily Kos.* http://www.dailykos.com/

Hoffman, B. (2006) *Inside Terrorism.* New York, N.Y.: Columbia University Press.

MacNab, JJ. (13 Feb 2012). What is a Sovereign Citizen? *Forbes Magazine.*

Muhlhausen, D.B., & McNeill, J.B. (2011). *Terror Trends 40 Years' Data on International and Domestic Terrorism.* The Heritage Foundation.

Ratcliffe, M., & Rabenstein, C. (2013). *Blackstone's Counter-Terrorism Handbook* (3rd ed.). Oxford, United Kingdom: Oxford University Press.

Russell, M.M. MAJ (2002). *Domestic Terrorism: Is America Prepared?* Quantico, VA: United States Marine Corps Command and Staff College.

Southern Poverty Law Center, The. https://www.splcenter.org/

Steven, G., & Gunaratna, R. (2004). *Counterterrorism.* Santa Barbara, CA: ABC-CLIO, Inc.

U.S. Government Publishing Office. https://www.gpo.gov

U.S. Nuclear Regulatory Commission. (2012 December). *Fact Sheet on Dirty Bombs.*

U.S. State Department. https://www.state.gov/

United Nations Office for Disarmament Affairs. *Biological Weapons.* https://www.un.org/disarmament/wmd/bio/

Wikipedia. https://en.wikipedia.org/

Wong, F.D. MAJ (2011). *Christian Extremism as a Domestic Terror Threat.* Fort Leavenworth, KS: School of Advanced Military Studies United States Army Command and General Staff College

Knowledge Check

1) The threat posed by homegrown violent extremists is greater than that posed by international terrorists.
   A) True
   B) False

2) The preferred weapon of the international terrorist is the:
   A) Explosive
   B) Small arms
   C) Biological
   D) Chemical
   E) All of the above.

3) It is easy to create a profile of a lone wolf homegrown violent extremist.
   A) True
   B) False

4) A right-wing, para-military militia extremists usually target:
   A) Law enforcement
   B) Government officials
   C) Judges
   D) Internal Revenue Service (IRS)
   E) All of the above.

Security Training Center,® LLC.

Knowledge Check Answers

4) E
3) B
2) A
1) A